HEINEMANN STATE STUDIES

Uniquely
Delaware

Katie Moose

Heinemann Library
Chicago, Illinois

Designed by Heinemann Library
Printed in China by WKT Company Limited.

08 07 06 05 04
10 9 8 7 6 5 4 3 2 1

**Library of Congress
Cataloging-in-Publication Data**

Moose, Katherine.
  Uniquely Delaware / Katherine Moose.
    p. cm.—(Heinemann state studies)
Includes bibliographical references (p.) and index.
  ISBN 1-4034-4644-X (lib. bdg.)—
ISBN 1-4034-4713-6 (pbk.)
  1. Delaware—Juvenile literature. [1. Delaware.]
I. Title. II. Series.
  F164.3.M66 2004
  975.1'043--dc22

                                        2003025979

Acknowledgments
Development and photo research by
BOOK BUILDERS LLC

The author and publishers are grateful to the
following for permission to reproduce copyrighted
material:

Cover photographs by (top, L-R): Dave Bartruff/
Corbis, Joseph Nettis/PhotoResearchers, Lindsey
Hebberd/Corbis, Joseph Sohm/Corbis, AFP/Corbis

Title page (L-R): Courtesy of Delaware Tourism
Office, Kevin Fleming, Kevin Fleming; pp. 4, 5, 6,
19, 27, 29, 30, 37, 40 Kevin Fleming; p. 7 Dave
Bartruff/Corbis; p. 9, 20, 25, 38, 43T, 43B
Courtesy of Delaware Tourism Office; p. 10 Culver
Pictures; p. 11, 23 Courtesy of the Delaware
Historical Society; p. 13T Joseph Nettis/Photo-
Researchers; p. 13B, 16T, 26 Brad Glazier; p. 15T
Alamy Images; p. 15B Fred Whitehead/Animals-
Animals; p. 16B Courtesy of the Agricultural
Research Service; p. 17T Mervyn Rees/Alamy
Images; p. 18T Carmela Leszczynski/Animals-
Animals; p. 18B Courtesy of the United States
Mint; p. 21 Doug Houghton/Alamy Images; p. 24
Hulton Archives; p. 31 Comstock Production
Department/Alamy Images; p. 32 John A. Rizzo/
Getty Images; p. 33 McDonald Wildlife Photogra-
phy/AnimalsAnimals; p. 34 R. Capozzelli/
Heinemann Library; pp. 35, 36 Brad Glazier; p. 39
Goodshoot/Alamy Images; p. 41T Lindsey
Hebberd/Corbis; p. 41B Joseph Sohm/Corbis;
p. 44 AFP/Corbis

Special thanks to Jessica Elfenbein from the
University of Baltimore for her expert comments
in the preparation of this book.

Every effort has been made to contact copyright
holders of any material reproduced in this book.
Any omissions will be rectified in subsequent
printings if notice is given to the publisher.

Cover Pictures

Top (left to right) Delaware state flag,
Kalmar Nyckle, Winterthur, snow geese
Main Fort Delaware

Some words are shown in bold, **like this.**
You can find out what they mean by looking
in the glossary.

Contents

Uniquely Delaware

What does it mean to be unique? Unique describes anything that is different in an important way from everything else in the world, or something that is one of a kind. Delaware has many things that make it unique.

Delaware is unique in that it is called the First State and the Diamond State. Delaware was the first state to ratify the U.S. Constitution in 1787, thus becoming the first state in the United States. Thomas Jefferson, the third president of the United States, compared Delaware to a diamond or jewel, which has great value and can cost a great deal of money.

ORIGIN OF THE STATE'S NAME

Delaware received its name in 1610 when Sir Samuel Argall, an English explorer, sighted Cape Henlopen on the Atlantic Ocean. He named it Cape de la Warr for the first colonial governor of Virginia, Thomas West, Third **Baron** de la Warr. The name was later used not only for

According to legend the famous pirate, Captain Kidd, buried a chest of gold in the Cape Henlopen sand dunes during a visit in 1700 on his trip to the West Indies.

the cape but also for the river, bay, land, and Native Americans who inhabited the area.

MAJOR CITIES

Delaware has only three cities with populations more than 28,000 people. Wilmington, the largest city, has 71,000 people and is located in the northern part of the state. It is a port and industrial city. The city's north-south streets are named for trees, famous people, and presidents, while the east-west streets are numbered. Along the water-front are a 11.5-mile track and the First USA Riverfront Arts Center, which opened in 1998.

Wilmington was incorporated in 1731 and was originally named Willington.

Dover, the second-largest city, became the capital of the state in 1777. William Penn of Pennsylvania first laid out the town around a town green in 1683. At that time Delaware was part of Pennsylvania. The Old State House in Dover, built in 1792, is one of the oldest U.S. capitol buildings. Outside Dover is Dover Air Force Base, home to the air mobility command and the C-5 Galaxy transport, the largest plane ever built.

Newark, **chartered** in 1758 by King George II of England, was a market town for trading cattle and horses, and later it was a mill town. In 1951 the Chrysler Corporation built the Newark Assembly Plant, which was first used as a defense plant and later used to manufacture automobiles. Newark is also home to the University of Delaware, which was founded in 1743.

Delaware's Geography and Climate

Delaware is bordered on the east by the Delaware River, Delaware Bay, and the Atlantic Ocean. The state shares the Delmarva **Peninsula** with Maryland and Virginia.

LAND

Delaware is made up of two geographic regions: the Atlantic Coastal Plain and the Piedmont Plateau.

The Atlantic Coastal Plain is a flat plain with a few hills that runs for 2,200 miles from Cape Cod, Massachusetts, to the Gulf of Mexico. Along the coastal areas are salt-water marshes and swamps. The Great Cypress Swamp in southern Delaware once covered more than 50,000 acres. Along the

Water and forest are the dominant geographic features of the Atlantic Coastal Plain.

Atlantic Ocean are beaches that attract many visitors during the summer.

The northern part of the state lies in the Piedmont **Plateau,** which is made up of rolling hills and valleys. Delaware has the lowest average elevation of any state in the nation, only 60 feet above sea level.

The Delaware River is the largest river in Delaware and the longest river in the eastern United States. The river starts in New York state and is 300 miles long. It forms the boundary between Delaware and New Jersey.

Bombay Hook National Wildlife Refuge

The Bombay Hook National Wildlife Refuge near Smyrna is located on the Delaware Bay along the Atlantic Flyway, the route birds follow as they head south in the fall and north in the spring. The birds feast on horseshoe  crab eggs from the Delaware Bay, which has the largest population of Atlantic horseshoe crabs in the world. During the winter the refuge is home to the largest population of snow geese in the **continental** United States. More than 100,000 snow geese may flock here. In 1981 the U.S. Postal Service issued the Delaware Migratory Waterfowl Stamp, which has a picture of a snow goose.

CLIMATE

Delaware has a mild climate. During July the temperatures are about 80°F. During January the average temperature ranges from 31°F to 38°F. The sun shines about 240 days a year. The state accumulates about 40 to 46 inches of rain during the year. Snowfall averages about eighteen inches in the north and fourteen inches in the south.

Average Annual Precipitation Delaware

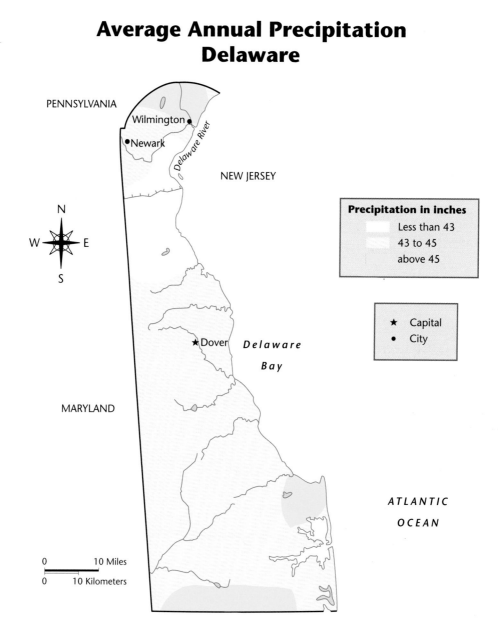

PENNSYLVANIA

Wilmington
●Newark

Delaware River

NEW JERSEY

N
W ✦ E
S

★Dover

Delaware Bay

MARYLAND

Precipitation in inches
Less than 43
43 to 45
above 45

★ Capital
● City

ATLANTIC
OCEAN

0   10 Miles
0   10 Kilometers

Famous Firsts

HISTORIC FIRSTS

In 1638 the first Swedish settlement in North America was established on the Delaware Bay at Fort Christina, near what is today Wilmington. The Swedes introduced log cabins. Most cabins had just one room.

The log cabin on exhibit at the Delaware Agricultural Museum in Dover dates from the late 1600s. The cabin was originally located in New Castle County.

On September 3, 1777, the U.S. flag flew for the first time during a battle of the American **Revolutionary War** (1775–1783). General William Maxwell ordered the Stars and Stripes banner to be flown at the Battle of Cooch's Bridge in Newark. This was the only American Revolutionary War battle fought in Delaware. Although the Americans lost the battle, they did slow down the British troops who were on their way north.

RELIGIOUS FIRSTS

Barratt's Chapel, built in 1780 in Frederica, is the oldest **Methodist** church in the United States. The church is built on land donated by Philip Barratt of Kent County. In 1784 the Methodists declared their independence from the **Anglican** Church of England.

INDUSTRIAL FIRSTS

In 1785 Oliver Evans (1755–1819) of Newport invented a flour mill that **revolutionized** the flour industry by allowing farmers to quickly grind corn. Before this invention, corn had been ground into flour by hand. Evans used shafts, gears, and belts to operate the machinery and a water wheel for energy. Elevators raised the grain up, while conveyors pushed it along. Hoppers then sifted and dried the flour. This type of flour was finer and could be stored more easily. He later built steam engines and boilers for boats, dredges, steamboats, and mills.

In 1832 the New Castle and Frenchtown Railroad operated the first passenger steam railroad in the United States. Before this time, horses pulled passenger coaches. Now a steam engine named *Delaware* was brought from England to pull the railroad cars. The ticket office is still located on Delaware Street near Battery Park in New Castle.

Oliver Evans' invention saved farmers time when they dropped off their corn. Instead of taking days to grind, Evans was able to do it in a few hours.

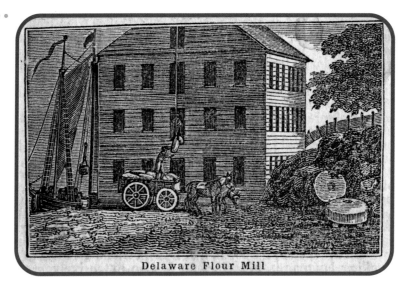

Delaware Flour Mill

Delaware's Shipbuilding Heritage

Shipbuilding has been an important industry in Delaware since the early 1700s. At that time all boats were built of wood. In the early 1840s Samuel Harlan of Betts, Pussey, and Harlan, makers of machinery, accepted a position on board the steamer *Sun.* He then founded the first iron shipbuilding yard in the United States. Iron ships are much stronger and the iron does not rot like wood does. This is important when a ship has to be in the water for a long time. The iron ore to make iron came from New Castle and Sussex counties. Forges were built to **smelt** the iron.

In 1844 the machinery firm Betts, Pussey, and Harlan became Betts, Harlan, and Hollingsworth and built *Bangor,* the first U.S. sea-going iron propeller ship. The Pussey and Jones Corporation, founded in 1848 by Joshua L. Pussey and John Jones, built the first U.S. iron-hulled ship, the *Mahlon Betts.* By 1868 Wilmington shipyards were producing more iron ships than anywhere else in the country. By 1880 only two shipyards still built wooden boats.

The Delaware **breakwater** at Cape Henlopen near Lewes was the first structure of its kind to be built in the Western Hemisphere. Between 1828 and 1835 rocks from the area were gathered to build a one-mile barrier to protect boats and the town of Lewes from the Atlantic Ocean.

In 1863 Job H. Jackson and Jacob F. Sharp founded the Jackson and Sharp Company of Wilmington to build passenger railcars and ships. In 1871 the company built the first narrow-gauge railcars in the United States for use in mountainous areas. Narrow-gauge rails have a shorter distance between the rails than do standard-gauge rails. This is necessary when building railroads in areas such as mountains to keep the railcars from falling down the steep slopes. The first order was for the Denver and Rio Grande Railroad.

CULTURAL FIRSTS

The first recorded beauty contest in the United States was held in Rehoboth Beach in 1880. This was at the time when women were beginning to wear bathing suits instead of long dresses to the beach. The winner of the contest was named "Miss United States" and received a bridal **trousseau.** Later this contest became the Miss America Pageant, which is held every September in Atlantic City, New Jersey.

The University of Delaware is one of the oldest colleges in North America. Founded as a small private academy in 1743, the university was formed in 1915 from the all-male Delaware College and the all-female Women's College of Delaware. Today, the university enrolls over 16,000 undergraduates and nearly 3,000 graduate students.

Delaware's State Symbols

Below the figures on the Delaware flag is the state motto "Liberty and Independence."

DELAWARE STATE FLAG

Delaware adopted the state flag on July 24, 1913. The flag has a blue background and a beige-colored diamond containing the state's coat of arms. The shades of beige and blue represent the colors in the uniform General George Washington wore during the American **Revolutionary War** (1775–1783). December 7, 1787, is the date that Delaware became the first state to ratify, or approve, the U.S. Constitution.

DELAWARE STATE SEAL

The state seal, adopted on January 17, 1777, contains the state's coat of arms. It also bears the inscription "Great Seal of the State of Delaware" and the dates 1793, 1847, and 1907. The dates 1793, 1847, and 1907 are the years the seal was changed. There are different symbols on the seal. The wheat, corn, farmer, and ox show that farming is important to the economy. The ship is a symbol the state's shipbuilding industry. The militiaman with his musket represents a soldier to protect the United States. The water stands for the Delaware River.

Images on the seal were adopted from those of New Castle, Sussex, and Kent counties.

State Motto: "Liberty and Independence"

The Delaware General Assembly approved the state motto "Liberty and Independence" in 1847. The words are used in the banner on the state flag and honor the American Revolutionary War soldiers who fought for the independence of the United States. Liberty means freedom, and independence means a person or country is able to survive on its own, with or without the control of others.

State Nicknames: First State

Delaware has had several nicknames over the years. It is often called the First State because Delaware was the first state to ratify the U.S. Constitution. President Thomas Jefferson called it the Diamond State or jewel because of its important location on the eastern seaboard. Delaware was known as the Blue Hen State when the mascot of the Delaware First Regiment during the American Revolutionary War was a blue hen chicken. This type of chicken was known for its ability in fighting other chickens.

State Song: "Our Delaware"

George B. Hynson wrote a poem titled "Our Delaware." The poem has three verses, one in honor of each of the state's three counties. Donn Devine wrote a fourth verse that praised the state and pledged the loyalty of its citizens. Will M.S. Brown set the poem to

"Our Delaware"

Oh the hills of dear New Castle,
and the smiling vales between,
When the corn is all in tassel,
And the meadowlands are green;
Where the cattle crop the clover,
And its breath is in the air,
While the sun is shining over
Our beloved Delaware.

Chorus

Oh our Delaware! Our beloved
   Delaware!
For the sun is shining over our
   beloved Delaware,
Oh our Delaware! Our beloved
   Delaware!
Here's the loyal son that pledges,
Faith to good old Delaware.

music. Delaware's General Assembly voted "Our Delaware" the state song in 1925.

STATE FLOWER: PEACH BLOSSOM

Delaware chose the peach blossom as its state flower in 1895. During the 1800s Delaware was a leading producer of peaches, with about 800,000 trees. Today, peaches are still grown in the state.

STATE TREE: AMERICAN HOLLY

The American holly tree, also known as the Christmas or evergreen holly, can reach a height of 60 feet. It became the state tree on May 1, 1939, because it is one of Delaware's most important types of forest trees.

Peach blossom flowers appear before peaches grow on the trees.

The American holly tree has dark thorny leaves and bright red berries.

STATE BIRD: BLUE HEN CHICKEN

On April 14, 1939, the General Assembly adopted the blue hen chicken as the state bird. During the American Revolutionary War, soldiers from Kent County under the command of Captain Jonathan Caldwell brought blue hen chickens with them as they fought in battles in White Plains, Trenton, and Princeton and on Long Island.

STATE FISH: WEAKFISH

Fishing is a popular pastime and important industry in Delaware. The weakfish became the state fish in 1981 because of its importance as a game and food fish.

Weakfish are also called sea trout.

STATE INSECT: LADYBUG

A second-grade class in Milford started a campaign to have the ladybug named Delaware's state insect. The state legislature chose the ladybug as the state bug on April 25, 1974.

Ladybugs are very small and are red and black in color.

STATE BUTTERFLY: TIGER SWALLOWTAIL

Three species of butterflies were selected as possible state butterflies. Students all over the state voted, and on June 10, 1999, the state legislature named the tiger swallowtail Delaware's official butterfly.

STATE MINERAL: SILLIMANITE

Delaware adopted sillimanite as its state mineral on March 24, 1977. Sillimanite is a glasslike mineral found in the northwest part of the state in Brandywine Springs and Hoopes Reservoir.

The large yellow-and-black striped butterfly is native to Delaware and can be seen throughout the state.

STATE FOSSIL: BELEMNITE

In 1996 belemnite became the official state fossil. The belemnite is an animal that lived in a shell a long time ago. It was similar to a squid. Belemnite fossils are found along the Chesapeake and Delaware canals.

Sillimanite can be used in jewelry, but it is not a precious stone like a diamond.

Shorebirds eat horseshoe crab eggs during their spring migration.

STATE MARINE ANIMAL: HORSESHOE CRAB

More horseshoe crabs are found in Delaware Bay than anywhere else in the world. In 2002 Delaware adopted the horseshoe crab as the state marine animal because of the marine animal's importance as food for shorebirds and in medical research.

DELAWARE STATE QUARTER

In 1999 the U.S. Mint began to issue new quarters. Delaware was the first state to have its own quarter. Congressman Michael Castle, a former governor, proposed the new coins, one coin for each state in the United States. Each coin has a picture of George Washington on the "heads" side.

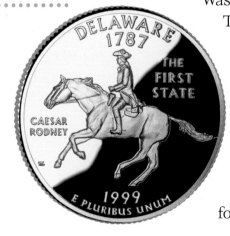

Caesar Rodney's horseback ride to the Constitutional Convention is shown on the Delaware quarter.

The Delaware coin has Caesar Rodney on the "tails" side. On July 1, 1776, Caesar Rodney was one of three representatives from Delaware at the **Constitutional Convention** in Philadelphia. He cast the deciding vote for independence.

Delaware's History and People

As one of the original thirteen colonies, Delaware has a rich history. Many people from all over the world, including Native Americans, Swedish, Dutch, and English, have made their homes in the state.

DELAWARE'S ORIGINAL SETTLERS

The earliest people to live in Delaware were two tribes of the Algonquin—the Lenni-Lenape in the north and the Nanticoke in the south. The Lenni-Lenape are one of the oldest groups of Native Americans in the United States. The name means "original people." The Lenni-Lenape wrote the oldest book in North America, titled the *Walam Olum,* or *Red Record.*

The Nanticoke lived along the Nanticoke River and Chesapeake Bay. Their name means "people of the tidewater."

SWEDISH AND DUTCH ROOTS

Henry Hudson of England was the first European to explore the Delaware Bay, in 1609. In 1610 another English person, Samuel Argall, sailed into the bay, thinking he was headed for Virginia. He named the area Delaware, and the Lenni-Lenape became the Delaware.

Traditional Lenni-Lenape clothing is made from tanned deer and elk hides.

Delaware was one of the first colonies in North America to be settled by Europeans in the 1600s. The earliest settlers came from the Netherlands and Sweden. In 1631 a group of Dutch formed a trading company to found a settlement along the Delaware Bay. Thirty people sailed on board the *De Walvis* (*The Whale*) and founded *Zwaanendael,* which in Dutch means "Valley of the Swans," the town of Lewes. Seven years later a group of Swedes arrived in what is now Wilmington. They founded the first permanent Swedish settlement in North America and named it New Sweden. In 1655 New Sweden became a Dutch colony called New Netherland.

ENGLISH COLONIAL HISTORY

In 1664 English warships captured New Netherland and made it part of New York. The Dutch captured it in 1673, but returned it to England in 1674. In 1682 King Charles II of England granted William Penn the province of Pennsylvania, which included the three "lower counties of Pennsylvania" that now make up Delaware. He named the counties New Castle, Kent, and Sussex.

The Delaware and Maryland Boundary

For many years the Calverts, an important British family who ruled Maryland, also claimed some of the land in the three lower counties that belonged to Pennsylvania. Taxes were collected by both colonies, which was a hardship on the colonists. In 1765 Charles Mason and Jeremiah Dixon, English **surveyors,** marked the boundaries to resolve the dispute. The boundary became known as the Mason–Dixon Line. The number "1" double stone marker, a one miler marker, was erected in Delmar, in southwest Delaware, in 1768.

Caesar Rodney

The Second Continental Congress met in Philadelphia to decide if the colonies should separate from England. Thomas McKean and Caesar Rodney wanted to declare independence, but George Read disagreed. On July 2, 1776, Caesar Rodney was in Dover and was sick. He received word that the voting was to take place, and he rode 80 miles on horseback to Philadelphia. He arrived in time to cast the deciding vote for independence.

THE AMERICAN REVOLUTION

By 1763 England decided to put very high taxes on some of the goods, including sugar, molasses, and tea, that it shipped to its American colonies. In 1765 the colonies had to provide housing and supplies for the British troops and to pay a stamp tax on all legal documents. The colonists did not like this. In 1774 the colonies decided to stand up against England. Delegates met for the First Continental Congress in Philadelphia, Pennsylvania, and petitioned King George III of England and claimed they had rights to "life, liberty and property." The three delegates from Delaware were Caesar Rodney, Thomas McKean, and George Read. They said they would remain loyal to the king.

In 1775 British soldiers fired on colonial soldiers in Massachusetts at Concord and Lexington. These were the first battles of the American **Revolutionary War** (1775–1783). Also in 1775 John Paul Jones was the first naval officer to fly the Grand Union flag, which later became the U.S. flag. The flag was on board the ship *Alfred* in the Delaware River.

The cottage where John Paul Jones was born is now a museum.

The first naval battle of the American Revolutionary War on the Delaware River between the British and the colonists took place on May 8, 1776. Two British ships, the *Roebuck* and *Liverpool,* fought several small U.S. boats and the Schooner *Wasp* off Christina Creek in Wilmington.

At that time New Castle, the capital of Delaware, and Philadelphia, capital of Pennsylvania, were located on the Delaware River. The British ships withdrew down the river and saved these two cites. The capital of Delaware was then moved to Dover.

STATEHOOD

On July 4, 1776, the colonies declared their independence from England with the **Declaration of Independence.** At this time Delaware also established a state government separate from Pennsylvania. Delaware was the first state to hold a **convention** to write a **constitution** after the signing of the Declaration of Independence in 1776. On December 7, 1787, Delaware was the first state constitution to be written by elected delegates, who were chosen from each of the three counties. The constitution was the document written by the citizens to establish their laws, rights, and freedom, independent of England. Every December 7th is celebrated as Delaware Day.

FAMOUS PEOPLE

John Dickinson (1732–1808), lawyer. John Dickinson was known as the Penman of the American Revolution. At the time of the Continental Congress, Dickinson spoke against declaring independence from England. However, once independence was declared he supported the decision. He wanted to help his country, and he drafted the original Articles of Confederation (1781), which established a new national government made up of the thirteen states. He was a signer of the Declaration of Independence and also served as governor of Delaware.

George Read (1733–1798), lawyer. George Read refused to vote for independence at the Continental Convention. However, when the resolution passed, he became a signer of the Declaration of Independence. He also served as governor of Delaware, was a member of the 1787 **Constitutional Convention** to write the U.S. Constitution, and was a U.S. senator.

Absalom Jones (1746–1818), minister. Born a slave at "Cedar Town" plantation near Seaford, Absalom Jones taught himself to read. Later, he attended a Quaker school in the evenings and eventually bought his freedom. He helped to establish the Free African Society in 1787. He became a leader of the independent African American church movement, and in 1792 he organized St. Thomas's African Methodist Episcopal Church in Philadelphia. In 1804 Jones became the first African American to be ordained an Episcopal priest. He opposed slavery and other forms of social injustice. He later became the first African American minister in the Protestant Episcopal Church.

Richard Allen (1760–1830), minister. Richard Allen was born a slave in Delaware. He, along with Absalom Jones, founded the Free African Society in 1787. He also founded the African Methodist Episcopal Church in Philadelphia and was its first bishop.

Thomas Garrett (1789–1871), merchant. Thomas Garrett, who lived in Wilmington, was strongly opposed to slavery. During the **Civil War** (1861–1865) he turned his home into the last stop of the Underground Railroad. The railroad was not a railroad, but a group of people who helped slaves escape to the Northern states or Canada for their freedom.

Thomas Garrett helped bring more than 2,000 slaves to freedom.

James Parke Postles (1840–1908), soldier. James Parke Postles of the 1st Delaware Volunteer Infantry Regiment fought at the Battle of Gettysburg during the Civil War (1861–1865). On the second day of the battle, he, under heavy fire, voluntarily delivered an order for the Bliss Farm to be turned over to the Union Army.

Annie Jump Cannon was the first woman elected an officer of the American Astronomical Society.

Annie Jump Cannon (1863–1941), astronomer. Annie Jump Cannon was born in Dover. When she was old enough to attend college, she became one of the first U.S. women to be educated beyond high school, and she graduated from Wellesley College, a women's college in Massachusetts. She later became an **astronomer** at Harvard University and divided the stars into different categories of brightness. She discovered more than 300 stars.

Eldridge Reeves Johnson (1867–1945), inventor. Born in Dover, Eldridge Reeves Johnson founded the Victor Talking Machine Company in 1901. The company developed the first record player, called a Victrola, which later became RCA Victor. The symbol of the company was a black-and-white terrier listening to his master's voice. The Johnson Victrola Museum in Dover has many old record players and recordings on display.

Henry Heimlich (1920–), surgeon. Born in Wilmington, Henry Heimlich developed the Heimlich maneuver in 1974 to save choking victims.

The du Ponts of Delaware

DuPont is one of the oldest and most successful corporations in the United States. DuPont is the largest chemical company in the world and the largest company in Delaware. The company manufactures nylon and other fabrics, dyes, medicines, and plastics.

MAKER OF GUNPOWDER AND EXPLOSIVES

The du Ponts, the most famous family in Delaware, settled in Delaware in 1802, the year E.I. du Pont founded Eleutherian Mills as a gunpowder and explosives factory. At that time gunpowder was not of good quality, but the du Ponts were chemists and developed better gunpowder for the government. The mill received its power from the Brandywine River. Willow trees along the river were cut to make the charcoal for the powder. By the time of the **Civil War** (1861-1865), Eleutherian Mills was the world's largest supplier of gunpowder.

Eleutherian Mills is located just north of Wilmington and is now a National Historic Site.

DuPont, located in Wilmington, is the sixteenth-largest company in the United States.

BETTER LIVING THROUGH CHEMISTRY

By the early 1900s the company had bought most of the other gunpowder companies. The U.S. government decided DuPont was too big, because DuPont's large size created a **monopoly** on gunpowder. Therefore, employees formed two new gunpowder companies. DuPont began to do chemical research and make paints, plastics, dyes, and **synthetic** products. Synthetics are artificial products that can be produced cheaper and are more readily available than are those products made from such things as leather, silk, or cotton. DuPont's inventions include cellophane, Mylar, ammonia, Rayon, **Teflon,** Orlon, Dacron, Kevlar, and nylon.

Nylon

In the 1930s Dr. Wallace Carothers, a scientist at DuPont, invented a fiber to replace silk, which at that time was very expensive. Nylon, a synthetic fiber, was first used to make parachutes, women's stockings, and brush bristles. Today, nylon is used in carpets, diapers, jackets, sleeping bags, and many other products.

Delaware's State Government

Delaware's government is based on the state constitution that was adopted in 1897. It is the fourth constitution in the state's history. The government in Delaware is divided into three branches: the legislative, the executive, and the judicial. Delaware is the only state in which the legislature can change the constitution without the approval of the voters.

LEGISLATIVE BRANCH

Delaware's legislative branch makes the state's laws. The General Assembly is divided into a Senate and House of Representatives. The Senate has 21 members, who are elected for four-year terms. The House of Representatives has 41 members, and each member is elected for a two-year term. Senators and representatives can be elected for an unlimited number of terms.

The Old State House in Dover was built in 1792 and remained the capitol until 1933, when Legislative Hall was built.

EXECUTIVE BRANCH

The head of the executive branch is the governor. The governor is elected to a four-year term and can be reelected for one more term. The lieutenant governor takes over if something happens to the governor and also serves as president of the senate. The executive branch makes sure the laws are properly carried out. The governor appoints the **secretary of state,** judges, and members of the board of education.

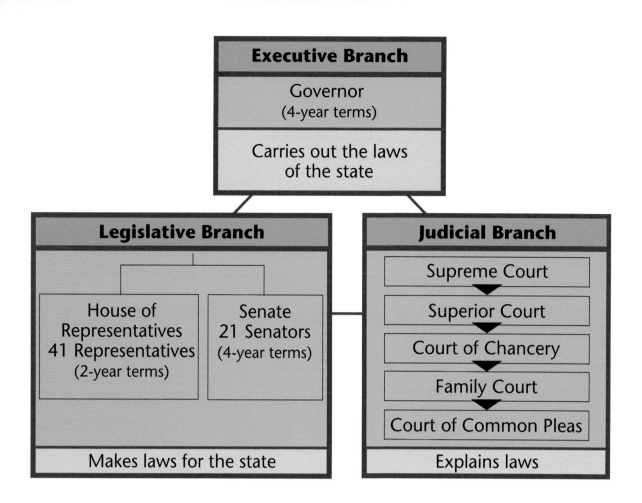

JUDICIAL BRANCH

The judicial branch is the court system of the government. The judicial branch interprets the laws through the court system. The Justice of the Peace Court handles minor criminal or motor vehicle cases and disputes in which the amount of money involved is less than $15,000.

Some of these cases may be taken for an appeal to the Court of Common Pleas. This court handles other minor crimes, except for drug or traffic crimes. The Family Court looks into matters that involve children or families. The Court of Chancery handles corporate issues, trusts, estates, and other financial issues.

The supreme court is the highest court. The chief justice and four associate judges are appointed by the governor and confirmed by the senate. They serve twelve-year terms.

Delaware's Culture

Delaware's culture is based on the environmental richness in the state. Many artists have been inspired in this scenic state.

THE BRANDYWINE SCHOOL

A group of artists, most of whom were **illustrators,** lived in Delaware and Pennsylvania. They were part of the Brandywine School, founded by Howard Pyle of Wilmington in 1903. The school is named for the Brandywine River that inspired many of the artists to paint idyllic scenes along the river. Their works can be seen in the Brandywine River Museum in Chadds Ford, Pennsylvania, the Delaware Art Museum in Wilmington, and the Samuel C. Biggs Museum of American Art in Dover.

Howard Pyle (1853–1911) was an artist who put action into pictures. His illustrations were done in a pen-and-ink style, but others were done in color. One of the last book covers he did was for Mark Twain's *Joan of Arc* and *Otto of the Silver Hand.*

The Brandywine river was named for a man named Andrew Braindwine who received a grant of land near its mouth in 1670.

Felix Darley (1821–1888) was an earlier illustrator from Clayton. His lifelike scenes done in pencil, ink, and oil led to his being called the "father of American illustrators." He illustrated Washington Irving's famous book *Rip Van Winkle and the Legend of Sleepy Hollow.*

A Day in Old New Castle

New Castle, once the capital of Delaware and the oldest town in the Delaware Valley, celebrates New Castle Day, which is the third Saturday in May. People dress up in costumes that are 200 years or older. Private homes usually closed to the public are open for tours. Other important buildings are the Old Dutch House, built in the late 1600s, and the George Read House on the Strand. The state's assembly met until 1777 in Old Court House, built in 1732. Packet Alley, located off the Strand, is where ships would arrive. It is named for the packet stagecoaches that carried goods to the boats for delivery to the people settling in the western part of the United States.

The city of New Castle, Delaware was founded in 1651.

Delaware's Food

A variety of food comes from the Delaware Bay or Atlantic Ocean, such as crabs and fish. Vegetables, fruits, and chickens are raised on farms.

BLUE CRABS AND CLAMS

Crabs are caught between April and May. Crabs can be steamed or made into salad or crab cakes.

Delaware's clams are called soft-shell clams, manni-nose, or steamers. The clams have thin shells and long necks that stick out of the shell, so it is easier to eat them after they have been steamed. Fishermen also use the clams as bait.

Soft-shell clams can be fried. The clam meat is coated with a cornmeal and flour mixture and then fried and served with tartar sauce.

Crab Cakes

Please make these crab cakes with the supervision of an adult.

1 pound crabmeat

2 tablespoons bread crumbs

1 egg

1 teaspoon Worcestershire sauce

1 teaspoon mustard

2 tablespoons mayonnaise

Dash of Old Bay Seasoning

Butter

With a fork, carefully combine the ingredients in a bowl. Shape into cakes. Sauté cakes in butter until brown on each side. Serve on sourdough rolls with tartar sauce and lemon. Makes four crab cakes.

SCRAPPLE

Scrapple has become a favorite breakfast meat in Delaware and Pennsylvania. Scrapple is made from ground-up pork scraps, spices, and cornmeal. When fried it is served in a sandwich or with eggs. Some people even pour maple syrup on their scrapple.

Delaware's Folklore and Legends

The word *folklore* describes stories that are told by one generation to the next over many years. The stories explain why something is done a certain way or why things look the way they do. A legend is a story that may or not have happened in real life.

WHY DOGS AND WOLVES DO NOT LIKE EACH OTHER

This Delaware Native American legend tells a story about a time when dogs and wolves were friends. During the winter the wolf said, "I am cold and hungry." He asked his friend the dog if he would get a stick with fire

from humans so they could have a fire. The dog went near to where the Delaware lived. He met a young girl who began to pet him. The girl saw the dog was cold and offered to feed him. He was so happy he went into her house with her. He forgot to bring back the fire. After waiting for a long while the wolf realized the dog was not coming back. That is why dogs and wolves do not like each other to this day.

CAPTAIN KIDD

Pirates often would look for buried treasure along the shores of the Atlantic Ocean or Delaware Bay. In the *Book of Pirates,* Henry Pyle tells how Captain William Kidd, a pirate, sailed into the mouth of the Delaware Bay with his crew in 1699. Tom Christ, a local boy, watched as pirates buried a chest in the Cape Henlopen sand dunes and then killed one of the pirates. He rushed off to tell the Reverend Jones. Together they traced the steps of the pirates and found a box filled with gold and all the pirate's papers. Those papers led to the capture of Captain Kidd in Boston. He eventually died in London.

Captain Kidd is supposed to have buried treasure chests in many other places besides Delaware.

Delaware's Sports Teams

Delaware is a small state but it has a number of sports teams. The Wilmington Blue Rocks, the University of Delaware teams, and others draw large crowds.

PROFESSIONAL SPORTS

The Wilmington Blue Rocks were a successful minor league baseball team formed in 1939. The team is now a Class A affiliate of the Kansas City Royals baseball team. The Blue Rocks play in Frawley Stadium in Wilmington, which also houses the new Delaware Sports Museum and Hall of Fame. In 2003 the *Sporting News* named former Wilmington Blue Rocks pitcher Zack Greinke its Minor League Baseball Player of the Year.

Frawley Stadium is named after former Wilmington Mayor Dan Frawley, who died in February of 1994.

Greinke began the 2003 season with the Blue Rocks and then went to Wichita.

COLLEGE SPORTS

The sports teams at the University of Delaware are called the Fightin' Blue Hens. The football team belongs to the Atlantic 10 Conference. They won the 2003 NCAA Division I-AA national championship. The women's lacrosse team won three consecutive America East Conference championships in 1997, 1998, and 1999. They also earned the team's first National Collegiate Athletic Association (NCAA) Tournament berth during the 2000 season. The basketball team was the America East Conference champion in the 1997–1998 season. The basketball team's best winning streak was twenty games in the 1991–1992 season.

The University of Delaware's mascot is a six-foot eight-inch blue hen named YoUDee.

Delaware's Businesses and Products

The chemical, automotive, and banking industries are Delaware's largest employers, followed by the tourism and agriculture industries. About one-half of the state's land is used for farming.

FARM PRODUCTS

Delaware's nickname "The Blue Hen State" is most appropriate for a state that has raised chickens since the first settlers brought them in the 1600s. During the 1920s chickens became a major industry. Today, Delaware is the leading producer of broiler chickens in the United States. The chickens received this name because they are very good broiled or cooked on a grill.

Sussex County in Delaware produces more than 200 million chickens a year, nearly twice the number of the second largest chicken producing county in the United States.

Cecile Steele

Cecile Steele of Ocean View started the broiler chicken business in 1923. She ordered 50 chicks, but instead received 500. She raised them until they were sixteen weeks old and then sold them. Because many of the other farmers in the state had diseased chickens, this sale was very helpful in starting the broiler industry. The shed in which Steele raised the chickens is now on display at the Delaware Agricultural Museum.

CRABBING

The blue crab is found in abundance in the mid-Atlantic region. More than 50,000 bushels are caught each year in Delaware waters, making Delaware fourth in crab harvesting in the United States. Commercial picking houses pack the crabmeat for shipping. Not all the meat can be used. What is discarded is ground up and added to chicken feed.

Blue crabs are abundant during the summer. They can be steamed or served as crab cakes, as salad, or in soup.

INDUSTRY

For more than 200 years, the gunpowder, chemical, paper product, and agricultural businesses have been important to Delaware's commerce. More than 300,000 companies are **incorporated** in Delaware, including half of the companies listed on the **New York Stock Exchange.** Incorporated companies usually have "Inc." after their name.

Since 1899 when Delaware passed its first corporation law, the state has always encouraged businesses to operate there. In 1981 Governor Peter du Pont signed the Financial Center Development Act into law. The law lowered the state income taxes that banks must pay. It also eliminated the limit on interest and fees that credit card companies could charge customers. Many banks moved into the state. The banking industry is now Delaware's number one employer, with more than 32,000 people. More than 60 percent of all credit cards are issued from Delaware banks. Eight of the top ten credit cards have facilities there.

More than 190 million people in the United States have a credit card. In 2002, they charged a combined total of 1.4 trillion dollars to their credit cards.

Attractions and Landmarks

Delaware is rich with history and has many attractions that draw visitors from all over the world.

LEWES

Lewes is located on the Atlantic Ocean in the southern part of Delaware. The "First Town in the First State" was settled in 1631 by Dutch settlers. It was once one of the busiest commercial fishing ports in the United States. The Zwaanendael Museum displays information on the fishing industry and Native American artifacts. The Cannonball House received its name because it was struck by a British cannonball in April 1813. Lewes is also a beach community. The Cape May–Lewes Ferry leaves from Lewes to take passengers to New Jersey.

Fort Christina was the first permanent Swedish settlement on the Delaware River.

FORT CHRISTINA NATIONAL PARK, WILMINGTON

The early Swedish settlers arrived on board the *Kalmar Nyckel* and

Reconstructing the *Kalmar Nyckel*

In 1986 a group founded the Kalmar Nyckel Foundation to design, build, and launch a replica of the *Kalmar Nyckel* at a shipyard adjacent to the original Swedish landing site. The boat was launched on May 28, 1997, and was commissioned in 1998. The boat has ornate carvings typical of ships of the 1600s, seven

working cannons, and masts that are ten stories high. It is a three-masted ship, is 139 feet long, and travels as Delaware's "Ambassador of Good Will," teaching about the history of Delaware. Other programs offered in the shipyard include wood-carving and blacksmithing skills, boatbuilding, and sailing.

Vogel Grip. They built a fort at "The Rocks" near what is Seventh Street in Wilmington in 1638. In the park is a replica of the *Kalmar Nyckel.* A short walk away is the Old Swedes Church, which was built in 1698 and is one of the oldest U.S. houses of worship in continuous use.

WINTERTHUR

The du Pont family, as they accumulated great wealth, built a number of grand estates around Wilmington. Among the largest is Winterthur, the former home of Henry Francis du Pont. He built the mansion in the early 1900s. In 1951 he moved into a smaller home and turned the house into the Henry Francis du Pont Winterthur Museum. The museum contains 170 rooms, each with a different theme. The Campbell Collection of Soup Tureens has more than 100 soup bowls. One room contains a pair of sofas owned by John Dickinson, a signer of the **Declaration of Independence.** Another room has 66 pieces from George Washington's dinner service.

Winterthur is located on 979 acres, and has 60 acres of gardens.

Places to see in Delaware

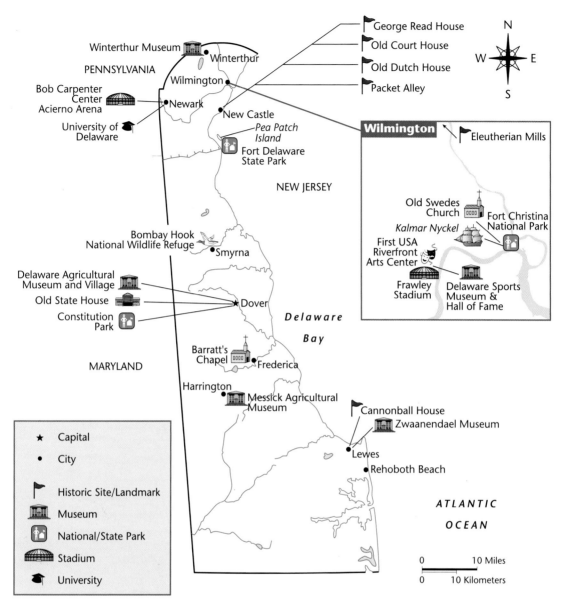

The Winterthur Museum has 985 acres of beautiful gardens. The Touch-It-Room at Winterthur has objects and activities for children.

THE DELAWARE AGRICULTURAL MUSEUM AND VILLAGE

The Delaware Agricultural Museum and Village in Dover traces the history of farming and communities in the state. The museum, founded in 1980, features farm-

The Delaware Agricultural Museum features more than 4,000 artifacts and fifteen historic structures associated with nineteenth century farming communities.

ing equipment, displays on dairying and poultry farming, and a Swedish log house in the exhibit building and Loockerman Landing Village. In the museum are a mill, train station, blacksmith and wheelwright shop, country store, barbershop, church, and old schoolhouse. Nearby in Harrington is the Messick Agricultural Museum, which has the first John Deere tractor on display.

Constitution Park

Constitution Park in Dover has a twelve-foot bronze **quill** that rests on a four-foot cube inscribed with the U.S. Constitution, signifying Delaware's being the first state to sign the U.S. Constitution. This is the only sculpture of this type on display in the United States.

The quill and U.S. Constitution are located near the State House in Dover.

Fort Delaware has 32-foot high walls and a 30-foot wide moat surrounding them.

FORT DELAWARE

Fort Delaware State Park is situated on Pea Patch Island in the middle of the Delaware River. The original fort was built in response to British aggression along U.S. coastlines during the War of 1812. The fort was finished in 1819, but a fire destroyed it. Many years went by before the new, stronger fort was completed in the 1850s. The fort served as a prison for Confederate soldiers during the Civil War (1861–1865).

The walls of the fort are made of thick bricks and granite. The fort has five equal or nearly equal sides and is three stories tall. Visitors can go inside the walls of the fort to the parade ground, which shows the officers' quarters, the mail and supply clerk's offices, the mess hall, and the staff offices. The museum inside showcases many artifacts and a scale replica of the island and fort during its Civil War prison years.

Map of Delaware

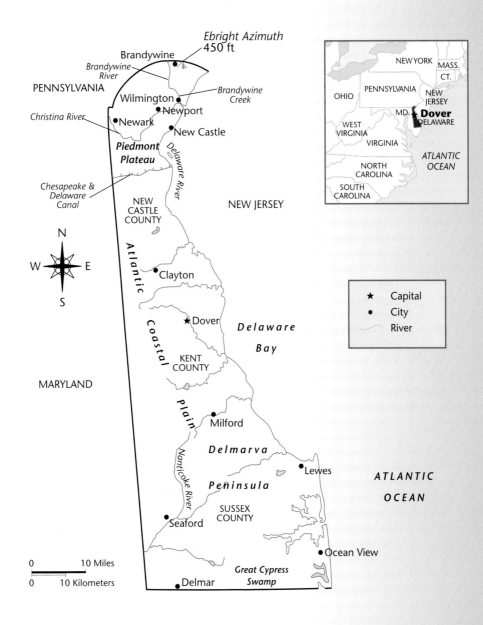

Ebright Azimuth 450 ft

Brandywine

Brandywine River

PENNSYLVANIA

Wilmington

Newport

Brandywine Creek

Christina River

Newark

New Castle

Piedmont Plateau

Delaware River

Chesapeake & Delaware Canal

NEW CASTLE COUNTY

NEW JERSEY

Atlantic

N
W   E
S

Coastal

Clayton

★ Dover

Delaware Bay

KENT COUNTY

Plain

MARYLAND

Milford

Delmarva

Nanticoke River

Peninsula

Lewes

ATLANTIC OCEAN

SUSSEX COUNTY

Seaford

0   10 Miles
0   10 Kilometers

Ocean View

Delmar

Great Cypress Swamp

NEW YORK   MASS.
CT.

OHIO   PENNSYLVANIA   NEW JERSEY

MD.   Dover
DELAWARE

WEST VIRGINIA

VIRGINIA

ATLANTIC OCEAN

NORTH CAROLINA

SOUTH CAROLINA

★   Capital
•   City
     River

Glossary

Anglican from or a member of the Church of England

astronomer person who studies the stars and skies

baron a man holding rights, lands, and a title directly from a king or other high-ranking nobleman

breakwater wall built to protect a harbor or beach

chartered when a monarch gives permission in a written document guaranteeing rights and privileges for land in a new country

Civil War the war in the United States between the Union and the Confederacy from 1861 to 1865

constitution written document that establishes how a state or country is to be governed

Constitutional Convention meeting in Philadelphia, Pennsylvania, in 1787, with delegates from eleven colonies to write the U.S. Constitution

continental states that are located on the North American continent, which does not include Hawaii

convention meeting of delegates with a common purpose

Declaration of Independence an act of the Continental Congress signed on July 4, 1776 which declared the British colonies in North America no longer belonged to England

illustrators artists who design pictures for covers and books

incorporated a company formed into a legal corporation

Methodist a member of the Protestant church founded in England in the 1700s on the teachings of John and Charles Wesley

monopoly company that has exclusive control of a product

New York Stock Exchange building in New York City where stocks of companies are traded

ornate having elaborate decorations

peninsula a piece of land that projects into a body of water and is connected with a larger land mass

plateau an elevated, level area of land

quill pen made out of a feather

Revolutionary War the war fought from 1775 to 1783 between Great Britain and the American colonies in which the colonies won independence

revolutionized radical change

secretary of state the head of the state government department that typically oversees the chartering of corporations and oversight of elections

smelt to melt iron ore so that it can be turned into a product such as steel

surveyors people who measure and describe regions, or parts, of the earth's surface, especially for use in mapmaking

synthetic something that is artificial or not made from the real thing

Teflon product made by DuPont that is often used in nonstick pans

trousseau a bride's personal outfit such as clothes and jewelry

More Books to Read

Blashfield, Jean. *Delaware—America the Beautiful Series.* Chicago: Children's Press, 2000.

Brown, Dottie. *Delaware—Hello U.S.A. Series.* Minneapolis, Minn.: Lerner, revised 2001.

Fradin, Dennis Brindell. *The Delaware Colony.* Chicago: Children's Press, 1992.

Fradin, Dennis Brindell. *Delaware—From Sea to Shining Sea Series.* Chicago: Children's Press, 1995.

Thompson, Kathleen. *Delaware—Portrait of America Series.* Austin, Tex.: Raintree Publishers, 1996.

Index

About the Author

Katie Moose is the author of six books. She lived in New Castle and currently resides in Annapolis, Maryland.